INSECTS
A PORTRAIT OF THE ANIMAL WORLD

Paul Sterry

NEW LINE BOOKS

Fax: (888) 719-7723
e-mail: info@newlinebooks.com

Printed and bound in Korea

ISBN 1-59764-126-X

Visit us on the web!
www.newlinebooks.com

PHOTO CREDITS
Photographer/Page Number

James H. Carmichael, Jr. 6, 13 (top), 15, 22, 23, 26 (top), 27, 37 (top),
42 (center), 43, 48, 52, 53 (bottom), 55 (top), 59, 60, 61 (top), 63

E. R. Degginger 10, 13 (bottom), 14, 16, 17 (bottom), 18, 21 (top), 28, 29 (bottom),
34 (bottom), 45 (bottom), 46 (top and bottom), 47, 66 (bottom), 68, 69 (top), 70

Phil Degginger 33 (top)

Dembinsky Photo Associates
Claudia Adams 51
John Gerlach 7
Doug Locke 69 (bottom)
Gary Meszaros 36
John Mielcarek 11 (bottom)
Skip Moody 3, 8–9, 32, 38 (bottom), 39, 44, 66 (top)
Stan Osolinski 71
Rod Planck 4, 21 (bottom)

Brian Kenney 5, 11 (top), 12, 19, 20, 24–25, 31, 34 (top), 35, 37 (bottom), 40–41, 42 (top),
45 (top), 50 (top and bottom), 54, 56–57, 58, 61 (bottom), 62

Nature Photographers Ltd.
Paul Sterry 17, 33 (bottom), 49, 64

E. S. Ross 30, 38 (top), 42 (bottom), 53 (top), 55 (bottom)

Tom Stack and Associates
Mike Bacon 67 (top)
Mary Clay 26 (bottom)
David M. Dennis 29 (top), 65
George Dodge and Dale Thompson 67 (bottom)

INTRODUCTION

Adult beetles characteristically have their first pair of wings modified to form hard wing cases which often bear a metallic sheen. At rest, the wing cases protect the second, fully functional pair of wings.

As the sun sets over a clearing in the Amazon rainforest, the last of the day-flying insects heads for the shelter of trees. A faint buzzing heralds the arrival of the first of mosquitoes that make up the vanguard of the nocturnal. The dark shapes of large moths and beetles reveal themselves but it is not until a lamplight glows that a clear idea of the amazing diversity of the forest's insects is visible. Thousands of moths, beetles, cicadas, mantids and bugs move toward the light. The air is thick with the sound of their clattering and whirring wings.

The tropics are, without doubt, the place to see a staggering range of insects. Their numbers and diversity, however, are still impressive in more temperate regions. Their abundance may be seasonal and the size of the largest specimens less imposing, but an interested eye cannot fail to be impressed.

Insects are by far the most populous group of animals on earth. Scientists now know of more than a million species in existence and estimate a total of up to thirty million more yet undiscovered species.

The secret of their success lies in their structure. They have a tough, protective outer skeleton and joints that allow for flexibility.

Above all, many insects have the ability to fly which helps them to escape danger, find new sources of food, colonize new areas, and expand their ranges.

The innate advantage of insects over many other invertebrate groups coupled with the adaptability of the group as a whole, has enabled them to colonize a wide range of habitats. Woodlands, forests, grasslands, deserts, and freshwater all have their quota of insects as do mountains, up to and including the snow line, and soils. The marine environment, home to fish, mollusks, and crustaceans, is the only place that insects have not exploited successfully.

The tough outer skeleton so characteristic of insects not only protects them in life, but has provided a telling fossil record of their past. Dragonflies with wingspans of more than 2 feet have been preserved in coal measures, and records of insects date back at least 350 million years. Unfortunately, this is not the case with soft-bodied groups of invertebrates. Interestingly, fossil records suggest that insects really began to diversify when flowering plants began to evolve.

The young nymphal stage of this grasshopper has a dusting of pollen from the orange hawkweed flower on which it is sunning itself. The powerful hind legs are characteristic of this group of insects.

Insects have developed an armory of means for disguising their presence from predators. As their name suggests, these thornbugs closely resemble plant thorns and thus escape detection.

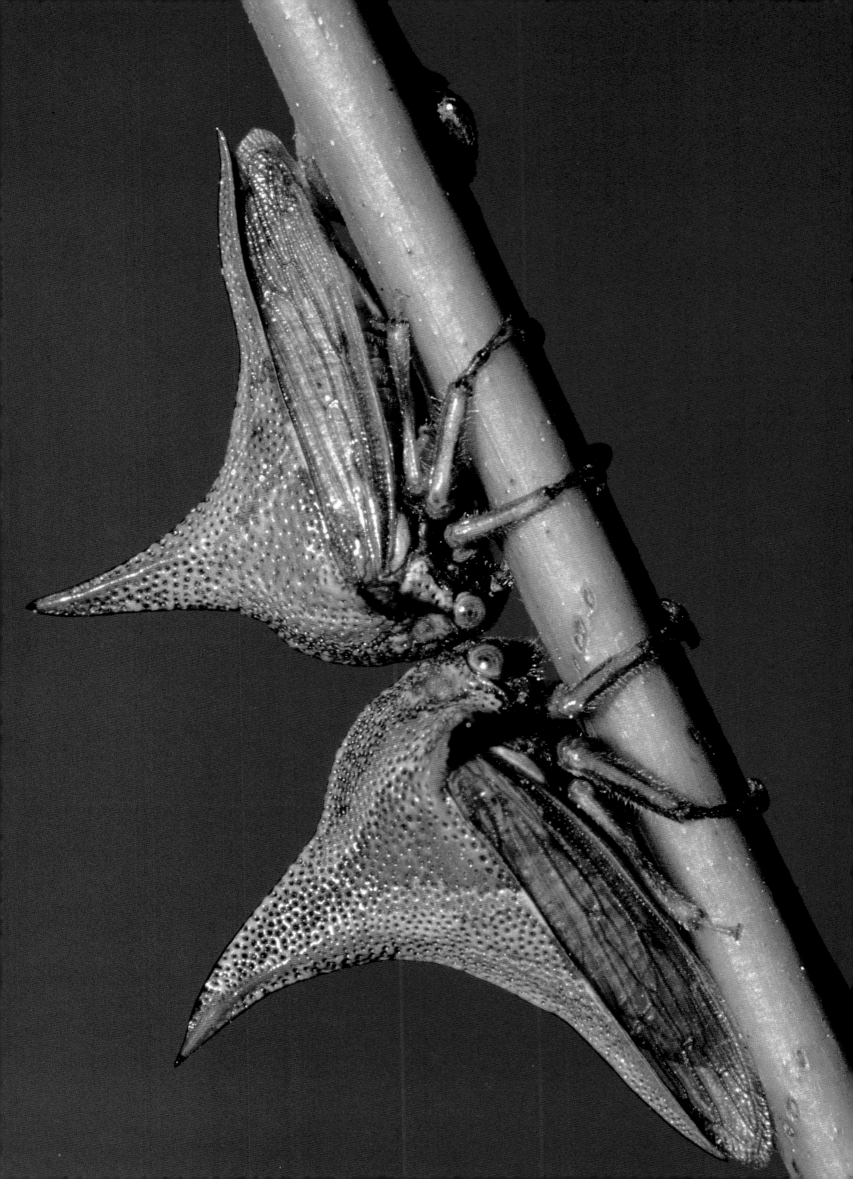

WHAT IS AN INSECT?

Insects come in all shapes and sizes from tiny fleas to moths that are larger than some birds. Despite this amazing variety, it is usually fairly easy to determine whether an animal is an insect or not. The presence of wings is a diagnostic feature in many adults because no other group of invertebrates possesses this characteristic or the ability to fly. Even without the wings, any creature with three pairs of legs is almost certainly an insect.

Insects in the animal kingdom

Scientists group animals together according to whether or not they have characteristics in common. The name of this classification arrangement is taxonomy. The main groups within the animal kingdom are Phyla (singular Phylum). Animals with backbones, such as fish, amphibians, reptiles, birds, and mammals are in a single Phylum often referred to as the Chordates. Animals without backbones (invertebrates) and simple animals are in an array of other Phyla.

One of the most important of the invertebrate Phyla, and the one to which the insects belong, is the arthropods. Members include crustaceans, spiders, millipedes, and centipedes. All of these have a hardened outer skin or exoskeleton, jointed legs and some degree of segmentation in the bodies. In terms of species, arthropods easily outnumber all the rest of the animal kingdom.

Insect classification

The body of an adult insect has three distinct sections. At the front end is the head which bears the mouthparts, eyes, and sensory antennae. Next is the thorax which carries the three pairs of legs and, in winged insects, the two pairs of wings. An immature insect does not have functional wings and, in some insects, nor does the adult. In primitive groups, these have never evolved and in more advanced insects they have been secondarily lost through evolution. The third section of the body is the abdomen; this has

Following page: This mating pair of promethia moths (Callosamia promethia) will remain joined at the tip of the abdomen for an hour or more. The larger abdomen size of the female moth (right) enables her to produce large numbers of eggs.

Dew-laden and inactive, this dragonfly displays the symmetry found in all insects. Transparent wings like these allow us to study the intricate venation which helps support these otherwise delicate structures.

This Costa Rican damselfly illustrates many of the most characteristic features of an insect. The three pairs of legs, two pairs of wings and segmented abdomen can be clearly seen.

segments and contains many of the insect's vital internal organs.

Entomologists—scientists who study insects—place them in a subdivision of the arthropods called a class. Within the whole class, insects with characteristics in common are further distinguished by orders. All orders, except the most primitive, are familiar to naturalists and have common names.

The many orders of insects fall into three categories. The insects of the first category do not undergo any kind of metamorphosis, are wingless, and are considered primitive. Only four orders fall into this category. The remaining orders comprise mostly insects whose adults have wings and some insects whose adults have lost their wings as a result of evolution. These winged orders fit into the second and third categories. The second comprises insects whose life-cycles involve only partial metamorphosis, and the third

includes insects that undergo a complete metamorphosis.

Primitive Wingless Insects
The four most primitive orders of insects are wingless and their small size and retiring habits make them easy to overlook.

Order Thysanura. Bristletails, silverfish and allies are in this order of insects whose bodies are covered with scales. They bear long antennae, and have short legs and three long bristles or cerci at the tail end.

Order Diplura. These soft-bodied insects have two cerci at the tail end. They are sometimes called two-tailed bristletails.

Order Collembola. These tiny, squat insects are able to leap by means of a sprung lever at their tail end, and are commonly called springtails.

Order Protura. There is no common English name for these minute, soil-dwelling insects that lack eyes and antennae.

In terms of appearance, weevils (Curculionidae) are *among the most extraordinary of all beetles. The blue coloration of this painted weevil only adds to the creature's visual impact on the observer.*

The green and black colors of this tortoise beetle from Amazonian Peru provide excellent camouflage when resting on a leaf. The splayed, translucent margin helps minimize tell-tale shadows.

This mud-dauber wasp is visiting a flower to collect nectar and inadvertently carries pollen with when it leaves. If it visits another flower of the same species, there is a good chance that cross-fertilization will take place.

An aptly-named harlequin beetle from South America rests on the bark of a tree. The soft-bodied larval stage of this insect bores into wood and thus protects itself from the attacks of predators.

This really is an insect and not just a jumbled assortment of dead twigs and leaves! If this giant stick insect's camouflage fail it, the spines that cover its body will deter all but the most determined of predators.

Many species of butterflies have eye-markings on their wings, but few are so striking or life-like as those found on the owl butter-flies of Central and South America. The false eyes help confuse would-be predators.

Insects With Partial Metamorphosis

Many orders of insects undergo a partial metamorphosis—their non-adult stages involve an egg and a succession of nymphs.

Order Ephemeroptea. Commonly known as mayflies, these primitive winged insects are the only ones that molt after they have acquired their functional wings. Most adult mayflies have two pairs of wings. The nymphs live in water and breathe through gills.

Order Odonata. This order consists of dragonflies and damselflies. Adults have two pairs of membranous wings. The head has biting mouthparts and large compound eyes and the abdomen is long and colorful. The nymphs live in water and are fierce predators.

Order Plecoptera. Known as stoneflies, these insects are rather flat. Adults have two pairs of membranous wings that they hold flat over the abdomen during rest. Their flight is weak. The nymphs live in water.

Order Orthoptera. This order includes crickets, bush-crickets, grasshoppers and allies. These insects' last pair of legs is modified and often enlarged for jumping. Many members of the order have hind wings particularly well developed for

flight. Female crickets and bush-crickets have elongated ovipositors at the tail end with which they lay their eggs.

Order Phasmida. We know these insects by their amazing mimicry of twigs and foliage. Long-bodied insects in this order are commonly called stick insects, and flat-bodied insects are called leaf insects.

Order Dermaptera. Commonly known as earwigs, adults in this order have distinctive pincer-like cerci at the tail end. The first pair of wings is short and not used in flight; the second pair is elaborately folded when at rest.

Order Embioptera. Called web-spinners, these slender insects have a swollen joint in each of the front legs, and live in soil and leaf-litter. The females are always wingless, the males sometimes so.

Order Dictyoptera. Cockroaches—insects with flattened bodies, long antennae, and spiny legs are in this group. Some species have adapted to live alongside human beings.

Order Isoptera. Commonly called termites, these are social insects with separate castes comprising fertile kings and queens and sterile soldiers and workers. They are able to feed on and digest wood.

Order Psocoptera. These insects are book lice or psocids—small, squat insects that live under bark or in books. Many species are entirely wingless.

Order Mallophaga. These biting lice are wingless parasites that often feed on birds and mammals. They have short legs and mouthparts adapted for biting.

Order Anoplura. These flat-bodied sucking lice have mouths designed to pierce and suck, and clawed legs for gripping. All sucking lice are parasites of mammals.

Order Hemiptera. These are true bugs—insects with piercing and sucking mouthparts. In winged varieties, two pairs of wings are present. The order has two distinctive sub-orders, the Heteroptera, which have forewings divided into a hardened base and a membranous tip, and the Homoptera whose forewings, if present, are wholly membranous.

Order Thysanoptera. These tiny insects, known as thrips, have fringed wings and sucking mouthparts used to feed on plants.

The life cycles of most insects are extraordinary but few more so than the seventeen-year cicada (Magicicada septendecim). As its name suggests, the young stages spend seventeen years underground, after which time the adults emerge in synchrony.

The head of an adult insect, such as this lumber grasshopper (Brachystola magna), possesses an array of sensory appendages included paired compound eyes, antennae, and palps surrounding the complex mouthparts.

Insects With Complete Metamorphosis

The third category comprises insects that undergo a complete metamorphosis from an egg, to a larva, to a pupa during their non-adult stages. These life-cycles are described in greater detail in a later chapter.

Order Neuroptera. This order includes lacewings, alder flies, snake flies and allies. Adults have large membranous wings with a complex network of supporting veins.

Order Mecoptera. Commonly called scorpion flies, these insects have slender bodies and mouthparts elongated to form a rostrum. The wings are membranous and held flat when at rest. The tip of the abdomen in males is swollen and resembles the sting of a scorpion.

Order Lepidoptera. Commonly known as butterflies and moths, these insects have large wings covered with scales, which are often colorful and conspicuously patterned. They have well-developed eyes and antennae and mouthparts modified to form a sucking proboscis.

Order Trichoptera. Known as caddis flies, these insects are superficially similar to moths, but have hairy wings that they hold like tents over their abdomens when at rest. The antennae are long and thread-like. The aquatic larvae often construct a protective shelter in which to live.

Order Diptera. These are true flies—a diverse group of insects that have a single pair of functional wings. Their greatly reduced hind wings help with balance. Adults have well-developed eyes and mouthparts modified for either piercing, sucking, or lapping liquids.

Order Siphonaptera. Commonly known as fleas, these laterally flattened insects have piercing mouthparts adapted to feed solely on blood.

Order Hymenoptera. This extremely diversified order includes bees, wasps, ants, sawflies and allies.

Many of these are highly social. In winged members, the two pairs of wings are membranous. There is usually a conspicuously narrow 'waist' between the thorax and the abdomen.

Order Coleoptera. These are beetles—a varied group of insects characterized by forewings that are hardened to form cases, called elytra, that protect the functional hind wings. The head bears biting mouthparts, well-developed eyes and, often, long antennae.

The water boatman spends most of its life in water, usually just below the surface. It can detect the distress movements of other insects trapped in the surface film and attacks them with its piercing mouthparts.

The bizarre appearance of this ghost walker beetle from Indonesia gives it more than a passing resemblance to a tropical seed. The paired antennae and three pairs of legs can be clearly seen.

The bodies of most adult insects, such as this field cricket, are covered by a hard outer casing called an exoskeleton, which helps reduce water loss and protects the soft tissues inside from damage and attack.

The eye-markings on the upper wings of this peacock butterfly can startle a potential predator such as a bird. Any resulting delay in attack may just give the insect sufficient time to escape.

Locked in a deadly embrace, this robber fly has just caught a smaller fly. The attacker's sharp mouthparts pierce the body of the prey, allowing its body fluids and soft tissues to be sucked up.

Body structure

Although appearances among adult insects vary greatly, their bodies remain organized in a manner common to all, irrespective of size or shape. There are three main sections: the head, the thorax and the abdomen. Each of these plays an integral role in the functioning of the whole animal.

The head. Although, anatomically speaking, there are six segments in the structure of the head, it is, to all intents, a fused, single structure at the front end of an insect's body. Paired compound eyes dominate the external appearance of many insect heads. Unlike human eyes, these comprise thousands of tiny cells called ommatidia. Each ommatidium is a visual unit with a lens and sensory cells. The insect's brain processes and interprets these multiple images. A close look at the surface of the head may reveal other light-sensitive ocelli as well as hairs that convey touch.

The antennae. The antennae also serve vital functions to an insect. They detect odor, temperature, and humidity among other things. The mouthparts are on the lower surface of the head and generally comprise three pairs of segmented appendages. The shape of the mouthparts varies considerably from order to order, reflecting the varied dietary functions they serve. Insect feeding and mouthparts are discussed in greater detail in a later chapter.

The thorax. An insect's thorax has three segments, each containing a hardened dorsal plate and a softer ventral region. Each thoracic segment bears a pair of legs and the latter two may or may not each have a pair of wings depending on the insect.

The abdomen. An insect's abdomen usually has obvious segments. In most groups there are typically eleven segments. Legs are never present on the abdomen but there are often appendages called cerci present at the tail end. The exoskeleton covering the abdomen is usually soft and flexible compared to that covering the head and dorsal surface of the thorax.

This close-up view of the compound eye of an insect reveals a mosaic of six-sided cells or ommatidia. Each records a separate image of the world around it, which the insect's brain processes together.

In certain lights, stunning iridescent patterns can be seen on the surfaces of compound eyes of horseflies. Close scrutiny reveals the thousands of small cells, or ommatidia, which make up the eyes.

21

The internal organs

Inside an insect's head, there is a rudimentary brain that receives information from the eyes, antennae, and mouthparts through a system of nerves. Other parts of the body are also in contact with the brain through a nervous system comprising nerve fibers and collections of nerve cells called ganglia located throughout the body.

Although the digestive system of an insect is, at its simplest level, a straight tube, there is considerable differentiation along its length. A crop serves to store food while the gizzard helps grind it down into digestible particles. The mid gut, off which there are sometimes outgrowths called caecae, is responsible for digestion proper, while the hind gut manages water absorption and excretion of waste.

A network of tubes called tracheae carries out respiration in insects. These tracheae open to the air via spiracles seen along the side of the thorax and abdomen. The tracheae branch and penetrate deep into the body. The heart circulates the blood, which bathes the body organs. The blood functions more for the transport and removal of food and excretory products than it does for respiration.

The exoskeleton, growth and molting

The exoskeleton of an insect is tough and resilient. It not only gives the animal its shape, but protects the soft tissues within from predators and excessive water loss. The exoskeleton is made from chitin and sclerotin. It may be soft and flexible in some areas of the body but hardened and rigid in others.

A tough exoskeleton has both advantages and drawbacks to an insect. Were it not for the sophisticated arrangement of the articulations in the leg joints and the soft nature of the exoskeleton in those joints, the exoskeleton could potentially restrict the animal's movement. The other main potential disadvantage is that it may restrict growth. To overcome this, the larval and nymphal stages of insects undergo periodic molts where the old exoskeleton splits revealing from within, a soft and ultimately larger one. Before the new exoskeleton hardens, the insect expands its body with air to accommodate the anticipated increase in size.

The swollen front legs of this mantidfly (Mantispidae), folded in the manner of prayer, helped to give the insect its name. The proportionately small, triangular head only adds to its praying mantid-like appearance.

The color and shape of this Malaysian leaf insect afford it superb camouflage. The effect is further enhanced by the presence of convincing-looking leaf veins and nibbled leaf margins.

LIFE CYCLES AND REPRODUCTION

The life cycles of insects have intrigued and fascinated naturalists for centuries because of their complexity. Indeed, were it not for the dedicated studies of skilled entomologists, the life cycles of many species would remain a mystery. The immature stages of many species differ so markedly from the adults that it is often hard to believe they belong to the same species at all.

The key to these unusual life cycles is insects' ability to metamorphose, that is to transform their appearance at various points in their lives. Most insects undergo life cycles with either partial metamorphosis—involving an egg, a series of nymphal stages and the adult—or complete metamorphosis—involving an egg, a larva, a pupa and the adult insect. These types of metamorphoses will be considered in more detail shortly. Among the most primitive insects, however, metamorphosis does not occur. Their development throughout life is simple and their life cycles will not be considered here.

Life cycles with partial metamorphosis

Examples of insects with partial metamorphosis are in taxonomic orders containing mayflies, dragonflies, crickets, grasshoppers, bugs and many others. Among some of these orders, the nymphs are rather similar to the adults but with others, the nymphal and adult stages are strikingly different in appearance. Whether or not the adult and nymphal stages are similar depends on whether they share the same environments: those that do share an environment, tend to look alike while those with terrestrial adults but aquatic nymphs, for example, differ.

The rather comical appearance of this mating pair of citrus root weevils belies the importance of reproduction in the lives of insects. Most species go to great lengths to ensure successful fertilization takes place.

Having found a suitable larval foodplant, this female tiger swallowtail (Papilio glaucus) has opted to lay a large number of eggs close together. Many other insect species choose to lay isolated and widely spaced eggs.

All insects, including those with partial metamorphosis, lay eggs. These come in an amazing array of colors, shapes and sizes and are laid singly or in clusters depending on the species. The case that encloses the egg is tough, but not airtight. Inside, there is a nutrient supply upon which the embryo relies for its development.

Insects often lay their eggs in a concealed place. Grasshoppers, for example, lay their eggs in the ground while female bush-crickets use their long ovipositors to inject eggs into the stems of plants. A few types of insects, such as praying mantids, go one step further and actually lay their eggs inside egg cases, or oothecae, which subsequently harden.

The term *nymph* describes the immature stage that hatches and develops from the eggs of insects with partial metamorphosis. As a general rule, nymphs show rudimentary wings that become proportionately larger throughout their molts. Because of their aquatic life styles, the nymphs of dragonflies and damselflies differ from the adults, most obviously in the presence of gills for underwater breathing. Terrestrial nymphs, such as those of grasshoppers, become increasingly like adults with each successive molt. They lack, however, functional wings and mature reproductive organs. Insects with incomplete metamorphosis do not have a pupal stage. Instead, the adult emerges after the final nymphal molt.

Life cycles with complete metamorphosis
Insects whose life cycles show complete metamorphosis are present in all the more advanced orders, including lacewings,

During the summer months, ladybugs from North America can sometimes be found gathered together in large mating swarms. Swarming behavior helps ensure that the chances of finding a mate are good.

To ensure successful fertilization, most insects remain paired for extended periods. During this time they are vulnerable to attack by predators, and so mating insect pairs often try to at least partly conceal themselves.

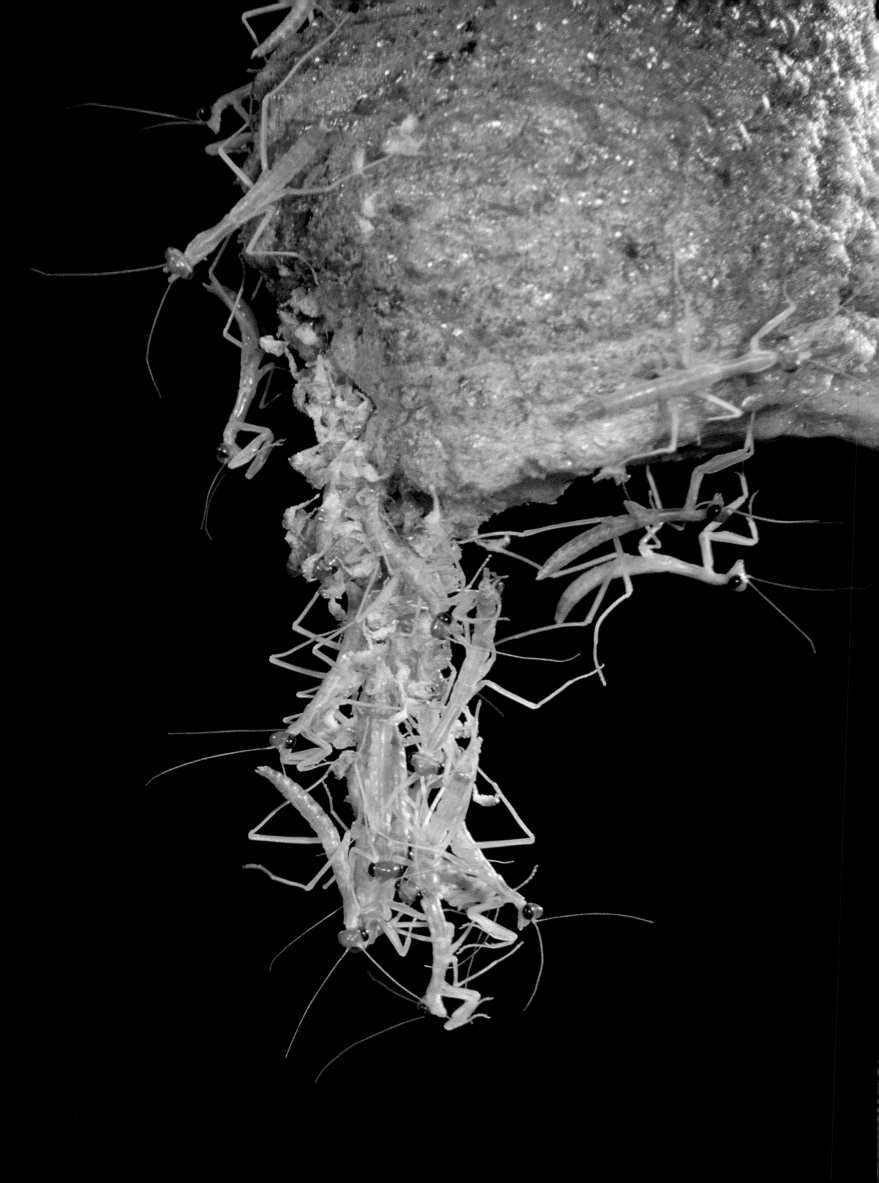

Cases of parental care are rare among insects. There are exceptions, however, as demonstrated by this male giant water bug lovingly carrying its eggs around on its back.

Following a development period of up to two weeks, these Mexican bean beetles larvae are just hatching from their eggs. Following emergence, it is common for insect larvae to consume at least part of their egg shells.

The eggs of a praying mantid (Mantis) are protected by a hard-coated case called an ootheca. Following their successful development within the eggs, the young mantids hatch and then emerge from the case.

Almost all insect larvae have well-developed heads with efficient mouthparts. This is essential to their main life cycle purpose of eating and growing. True legs, if present, are on the first three segments of the body. In butterfly and moth caterpillars and the larvae of sawflies, a number of sucker-like prolegs appear toward the rear end of the body.

Because caterpillars and larvae are generally soft-bodied and vulnerable to predators, they usually conceal themselves. Some show good camouflage while others live buried in the ground, bore into wood, or make protective cases in which to live. Parental care is comparatively rare in most insects except among the social insects, namely, wasps, bees, and ants.

The constraint of having an exoskeleton, albeit a rather soft one, means that larvae have to molt at regular intervals in order to grow. The individual larval stages between molts are *instars*. Although each instar may differ from the previous one in terms of color and markings, they are all easily recognizable as larvae.

After the final instar, the soft-bodied, active larva molts and metamorphoses into a hard-cased, inactive pupa. Prior to pupation, the larva often finds a protected site. In many species, this involves burrowing underground or creating a shelter from leaves or bark.

Many of the features of the adult insect appear in outline on the case of the pupa. In a butterfly pupa, for example, the well-developed head with compound eyes, proboscis, and antennae is clearly visible as are the wings and full-sized legs.

Although the insect may appear dormant during the pupal stage, it would be a mistake to think of this as purely a resting stage in the life-cycle. Inside the pupal case, most of the organs of the body are completely reorganized. Those appropriate to the larval stage fade away while those necessary for adult life appear.

Waste not, want not is the approach adopted by this female praying mantid. During the act of mating, she begins to consume her male partner, head first. His death ensures a rich supply of nutrients for the developing eggs.

butterflies, moths, caddis flies, true flies, bees, wasps, and beetles. In all cases, the four stages in the life cycle—the egg, larva, pupa and adult—are strikingly different from one another in appearance.

Following mating and successful fertilization, insects showing complete metamorphosis lay eggs like other insects. The eggs come in all shapes and colors, and share the fact that they are much smaller than other stages in the life cycle. Most species of insects lay between twenty and 100 eggs. The number depends on the species.

The term *larva* describes the immature stage that hatches from the eggs of insects with complete metamorphosis. This stage generally looks quite unlike the adult stage and is often grub-like and segmented.

When newly emerged from the pupa, the wings of butterflies and moths are soft and crumpled. This monarch (Danaus plexipus) is just starting to pump them up to their full size, after which they will dry and harden.

Battles of the sexes

Almost all species of insects have two sexes. The creation of a new generation requires the successful meeting and mating of members of the opposite sex. The often striking difference in appearance between males and females is called *sexual dimorphism*.

The male, in most insect species, goes in search of the female. Among the day-flying insects, where males and females often look quite different, the male may use visual signals, such as wing color and pattern, or behavior, to locate the female. For many other insects, females release a chemical attractant called a *pheromone* to help guide the male. Nocturnal insects often employ this technique but a few specialized ones, notably glow-worms and fireflies, have females that emit light signals to attract mates.

Having met, the male and female usually undergo a brief period of courtship. This helps to ensure that both are truly members of the same species and that both, the female in particular, are ready for mating.

Fireflies (Lampyridae) are perhaps the best known of all bioluminescent insects. Although their ability to emit light is fascinating when seen in close up, the sight of a whole swarm can be truly startling.

In some primitive insects, the male deposits' sperm into an external packet called a *spermatophore* that is then used by the female to fertilize her own eggs. In more advanced insects, coupling takes place with the tips of the abdomens linked during sperm transfer. In most species, the sperm is stored inside the female's body and the eggs are fertilized as she lays them. After mating has taken place, the male and female usually separate although in some insects, they

Measuring nearly 7 inches (18 centimeters) long, the larva of the death's-head sphinx moth (Acherontia atropos) is one of the largest of all moth caterpillars. The yellow coloration and purple diagonal stripes make it visually stunning as well.

This adult dragonfly (Odonata) has just emerged from the split skin of its nymph. At first, the body—particularly the wings—are soft and limp. Within minutes, however, they expand and harden.

Having just emerged from its egg, this tiny eyed hawkmoth larva prepares to enjoy its first meal—the shell of the egg from which it hatched. This provides it with valuable nutrients.

may remain paired until the female lays her eggs.

The strange lives of aphids

In certain types of insect, females can give birth to viable offspring without the need for male sperm. This process is *parthenogenesis*. Throughout the summer months, aphids produce generation after generation of offspring by this method. Most of these offspring are wingless but some are winged and can disperse. At the end of this season, however, separate males and females develop. These then mate in the manner of other insects and lay eggs that mature over winter to produce next year's stock of aphids.

Bioluminescence is rare in insects, but nevertheless spectacular when it does occur as with these New Zealand glow-worms. Generally, the function of bioluminescence is in some way related to mate attraction.

Having completed its growth, the larva or caterpillar of this monarch butterfly caterpillar is metamorphosing into a chrysalis or pupa. Look closely and you will see the larval skin splitting to reveal the pale green pupa.

FOOD AND FEEDING

Innumerable insects have evolved to eat almost every type of organic matter in existence. Everything from leaves and solid wood to the living tissues of mammals or decaying corpses is food for one insect or another. The success of insects in exploiting this vast range of food sources lies in their highly specialized mouthparts. Although the basic plan is quite simple, evolution has resulted in today's many designs. To survey insect diets, one must consider the shape and structure of the insects mouthparts, as well. For the student of entomology, this is all the more fascinating because larval and nymphal stages often have markedly different diets from adults of the same species.

The basic insect mouthparts plan comprises three pairs of segmented appendages. From front to back these are: a pair of mandibles, a pair of jaws or maxillae, and a fused pair of appendages that form a lower lip or labium. A plate-like upper lip or labrum protects the front of the mouth and helps direct food, as do the paired maxillary palps and labial palps.

The most common mouthpart adaptations

One of the most common ways in which insects feed is by chewing their food. Mouthparts designed for chewing are fundamentally similar whether the diet consists of plant or animal matter. The chewing mouthparts of carnivores do, however, tend

The mouthparts of most moths and butterflies have evolved to form a long proboscis. Coiled when at rest, this tubular structure can be extended at will to probe deep inside flowers for sugar-rich nectar.

The assassin bug is certainly well named. Even the nymph, shown here attacking a cranefly, is predatory and uses its long proboscis to suck the body fluids and soft tissues from the body of its victim.

Great diving beetles are among the most ferocious of all insect predators. They are powerful swimmers and will happily tackle large prey such as this larval salamander, or even small fish.

Once embraced by the praying mantid's spine-fringed legs, the fate of this hapless grasshopper was sealed. The mantid's powerful, razor-sharp mouthparts easily slice through the exoskeleton of the victim.

Insects that are poisonous or foul tasting, such as these beetles, often advertise the fact with bright warning colors. The toxins are often acquired from their foodplants or those of their larval or nymphal stages.

to be longer and thinner than those of herbivores.

At the other extreme, many insects have highly modified mouthparts designed for sucking up liquids. Depending on the type of liquid taken, many or all of the mouthparts are elongated to form a tube.

Varied diets and life styles

Leaves are among the most common dietary components for herbivorous insects with chewing mouthparts. The majority of butterfly and moth species have larvae (called caterpillars) which eat leaves. Newly hatched caterpillars from small species tackle the leaf surface and a few species, known as leaf-miners, actually live within the thickness of the leaf itself. Larger caterpillars generally eat leaves side-on as do the larvae of some beetles and sawflies.

Wood may seem too tough to penetrate and of little nutritional value for most insects but the larvae of many insects, beetles in particular, are well adapted to exploit timber. Some species favor dead wood or go just below the bark of living trees while a few can actually bore deeper into living wood. Ironically, most wood-boring insect larvae are elongated and soft-bodied, and rely on the wood into which they bore for protection from predators.

Sugar-rich nectar is another important source of food for many insects. Flowers produce this liquid in order to attract pollinating insects. In butterflies and moths, the maxillae form a long, tube-like proboscis, and the mandibles are absent.

The adults of many species of flies also imbibe liquids through the labium that evolves into a broad- and flexible-tipped proboscis for this purpose. It is only a short evolutionary step from these insects, that feed from pools of liquids, to those that pierce skin and drink blood. Horseflies and mosquitoes employ the latter feeding method.

Perhaps the supreme examples of insects with sucking mouthparts are among the true bugs. Many of these take advantage of the nutrient-rich sap that flows through living plants with their mouthparts. For this, the mandibles and maxillae are elongated and protected by a sheathing tube formed by the labium. Carnivorous bugs also use these piercing mouthparts to deadly effect, feeding on other invertebrates or attacking their fellow insects.

Keen eyesight enabled this giant robber fly to spot potential prey with ease. Having seized an unfortunate skipper butterfly with its all-embracing legs, the fly's piercing mouthparts will soon suck the victim dry.

Following page:
In the northern hemisphere, the months of August, September, and October provide the insect world with a bumper harvest of berries. This lubber grasshopper is feasting on the rich supply of sugars and other nutrients.

The mouthparts of this funny face katydid from Costa Rica are superbly adapted to deal with the tough leaves of rainforest plants. In a small way, the front legs assist in guiding the leaf in the right direction.

The narrow proboscis of this Costa Rican heliconius butterfly (Heliconiidae) can clearly be seen probing the center of a zinnia flower. In return for nectar, the butterfly will inadvertently transfer pollen from this flower to the next one it visits.

Some fast-flying insects, such as this spiderfly, possess the ability to hover in mid-air. They have dispensed with the need to land on a flower in order to feed on its nectar, using the long proboscis to drink nectar on the wing.

Although many insects simply visit flowers to collect nectar, this katydid clearly views this hibiscus flower's reproductive structures as a potential meal. Its powerful mouthparts will make short work of the plant's soft tissues.

MOVEMENT

Adult insects are among the most mobile and active invertebrates. All use their legs for movement; some move slowly and others at a great scurrying pace. A few orders have evolved the ability to leap, making use of powerful back legs, while others are effective swimmers both at the surface and underwater. The mode of transport that adult insects have made best use of, and the one unique to them among all invertebrates, is the ability to fly. Wings have liberated insects and helped make them the most diverse and numerous group of animals on the planet.

Structure and movement

Most adult insects have three pairs of legs. These attach to the underside of the segments of the thorax, one pair per segment. Although some species show modification, most insect legs comprise five sections. From the body outward, these are: the coxa, the trochanter, the femur, the tibia and the tarsus. The tarsus normally has several segments and is usually hooked at the tip. The angle at which each segment articulates with the next varies along the length of the leg, allowing for considerable flexibility and freedom of movement. There are muscles inside the exoskeleton of the leg segments.

Having grabbed its victim, a praying mantid will often eat it head-first. This rather gruesome approach ensures that the nervous system is severed, thus limiting the struggling activities of the victim.

The wonders of high-speed photography have helped capture the miracle of flight on film. At the point in this honey bee's wingbeat that the photograph was taken, the wings were angled towards the camera and hence appear invisible.

Some insect predators actively hunt their prey while others, such as praying mantids, use stealth and concealment to approach the unsuspecting victim. When within range, the grasping front legs shoot out at lightning speed.

Leaping

The front legs are smaller than the hind legs in most insect species. Among those which scurry or walk, the size differences may appear rather subtle, but for those with more specialized movement, it can be marked. Grasshoppers, for example, have proportionately large hind legs to accommodate bigger muscles in the femur. They can easily leap many tens of times their own body length to escape danger. There are always exceptions, however, in mole-crickets (*Gryllotalpa* sp) the front legs outsize the hind and are modified for digging.

Swimming

Although many aquatic insects are slow moving, others are more active and have developed a paddle-like fringe of hair on their legs to assist them in swimming. Among the water beetles, this fringe is usually on the hind legs while in the water boatman (*Notonecta* sp) it is on the front legs. Nymphs of dragonflies, which, unlike the adults, live aquatic lives, have an extremely novel means of propelling themselves through the water. When threatened, they expel water through the tip of their abdomen in a form of insect jet propulsion.

Special leg modifications

In some insects where the shape of the leg has something to do with a function other than movement, there are a variety of special leg modifications. Among the praying mantids (*Mantis* sp), for example, the front legs are modified for catching prey. They can shoot out quickly and have spines along their inner edge for gripping. Water stick-insects (*Ranatra* sp) have similar leg modifications. Honey bees (*Apis mellifera*) and many of their relatives have specially modified back legs for carrying pollen from flowers to the hive. Leg modifications are not always for feeding. Male diving beetles (*Dytiscus* sp), for example, have suckers on their front legs that allow them to grip the slippery female during mating.

In the insect world, movement is not always confined to air and land. Species such as diving beetle are adept swimmers and have specially modified, fringed hind legs to assist their propulsion.

A grasshopper's hind legs are its main means of propulsion as it hops away from danger. It is vital that the main joint on the legs is sufficiently robust to withstand the powerful forces exerted during leaping.

An insect's wings

As already mentioned, among the invertebrates, wings are unique to insects and the ability to fly has contributed greatly to their successful colonization of terrestrial habitats on the planet.

Unlike birds and bats, whose flight is powered by wings that have evolved from modified limbs, the wings of insects are separate structures from the legs. They are hardened outgrowths from the upper surfaces of the second and third segments of the thorax. The wings are powered by muscles attached at one end to the base of the wing inside the thorax, and at the other to the inner thoracic wall. A network of veins holds the insects' wings rigid.

Most adult insects have two pairs of wings although there are exceptions. Among the true flies, the reduced and modified hind wings are for balance rather than flight. With beetles, on the other hand, the hind wings manage flight while the fore wings form hard cases to protect the hind wings during non-flight.

Wing shape and color

Wings come in all shapes, sizes, and colors. Their appearance has much to do with the life style of the insect and any specific function required of the wings themselves. Butterflies, for example, often have broad, rounded wings that enable them to glide from one flower to another. Some moths and most flies have narrower wings more suited for accurate and sometimes prolonged hovering. The wings of moths and butterflies are covered in scales and often brightly colored or subtly marked. The colors and shapes help with a range of functions from species recognition to warning markings and camouflage. Where they seemingly serve no additional behavioral function, wings are often transparent.

The warming rays of the sun are enjoyed by many insects, such as this Malay lacewing butterfly. The heat absorbed by the body and wings will help speed up the metabolism of the insect's body.

The purpose of flight

Winged insects with even the most limited powers of flight invariably use their wings to escape from danger. Those whose flying skills are more advanced, however, use flight for a wide range of things from dispersal and feeding, to finding a mate and choosing a site to lay eggs.

Insects are impressive in both the speed at which they fly and, in a few species, their power of endurance. Some butterflies and moths undergo long annual migrations involving flights of hundreds, if not thousands, of miles. The painted lady butterfly (*Vanessa cardui*) is the best known European example. Each spring these head northwards in successive generations from their year-round haunts in southern Europe and north Africa. In the Americas, the monarch butterfly (*Danaus plexippus*) is equally famous. Monarchs spend winter in Mexico but each spring successive generations head north until they reach well into Canada. A reverse migration occurs in late summer and autumn until they reach their wintering grounds.

Although fast and active fliers, dragonflies spend long periods resting on waterside perches. From here they can watch for potential prey as well as for rival dragonflies entering their territories.

Winged insects such as this halloween pennant dragonfly have a wing venation unique to each species. For certain insect groups, entomologists use these arrangements of veins as a means of classification and identification.

Some flying insects, such as this Cynthia moth from southern Florida, are so large that they dwarf many of the birds found in the same region. For such sizable insects, flying expends an awful lot of energy.

Like other hawk-moths, this lesser vine sphinx has relatively narrow, pointed wings. These are ideally suited to the fast, active flight that characterizes this fascinating group of insects.

SELF–DEFENSE

With such diversity and abundance among insects, it is little wonder that these invertebrates are a favorite source of food and nutrition for many animals, including other insects.

A fair proportion of the world's terrestrial birds includes insects in their diet and some, such as warblers (*Sylviidae* and *Parulidae*), are almost exclusively insectivorous. In temperate parts of the world, the nesting of woodland birds coincides with maximum insect abundance because the birds' breeding success depends on the availability of food. Some species of mammals have similar insectivorous habits, too. Most bats, for example, feed exclusively on night-flying moths.

Predators of insects do not always have things come easily. Evolution has enabled insects to develop a varied armory to defend themselves. At the simplest level, leaping and flying help many insects escape danger but elaborate and sometimes subtle methods include poisons, chemical sprays and stings.

Insect armory
The hardened body casing of most adult insects is a useful deterrent to all but the most

determined or powerfully built predators. This is especially true where spines reinforce the defense. When provoked, some species, notably, the ladybirds (*Coccinella* sp) can defend themselves by retracting their rather delicate legs into grooves on the underside of the body.

Because the caterpillars of moths and butterflies are generally soft-bodied and slow-moving, they make tempting targets for birds and other insects. Many rely on remaining hidden from view but others take a more aggressive approach by defending themselves with hairs that irritate potential attackers.

The threat display of this valiant female praying mantid is designed to deter any potential predator from showing an interest in her egg case. If the threat continues, she will unhesitatingly launch an attack.

Seen out of context, this katydid looks bizarre. However, among a tangled mass of similarly colored lichens, it will be effectively camouflaged.

At first glance, this photograph shows a collection of mosses and lichens, not an insect. Look closely, however, and you will see a superbly camouflaged katydid from the forests of Ecuador.

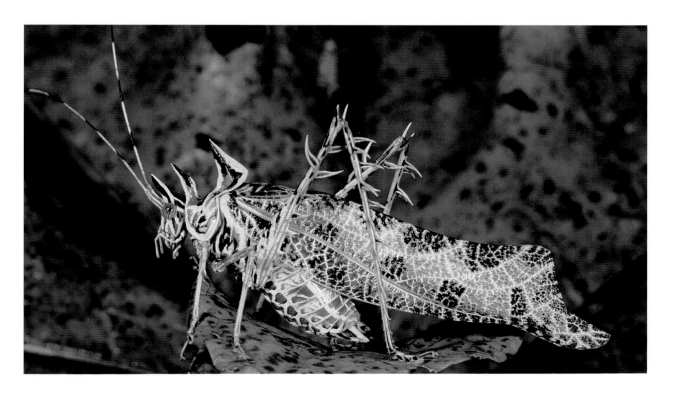

Physical defense

The most obvious way in which a predatory insect can defend itself from attack is by using its mouthparts to bite its attacker; this is, indeed, what most will do under these circumstances. In some species, the bite may be accompanied by the injection of potentially toxic chemicals, which are either contained in the saliva associated with their carnivorous diet or are present specifically for defense.

Chemical defense

Many bees and wasps defend themselves by attacking. In this case, the threat comes from the rear end of the animal, in the form of a sting shaped like a hypodermic needle. Although the penetration of the sting may cause some pain to a would-be attacker, the injection of poisons causes most of the agony. Stings are modified ovipositors and so only females can sting. While wasps can, and will, sting repeatedly, a bee's sting is usually lodged in its victim and torn from the insect's body thereby killing the bee.

Another intriguing means of chemical defense is in the bombardier beetles (*Brachinus* sp). When provoked, these ground-dwelling insects can emit a cloud of super hot gas from the tip of their abdomen. The temperature has the potential to cause severe irritation to the face of predators such as shrews or birds.

Poisons and warning colors

Many insects accumulate poisonous chemicals within their bodies which make them distasteful and, in certain species, actually make them toxic. In some insects, these chemicals are produced in the body but others, such as caterpillars, acquire the toxins from the leaves that make up their natural diet.

It is no use for an insect to be poisonous if a predator can mortally wound or eat the

The horn-like structures on this male rhinoceros beetle (Dynastes) from Trinidad are used in battles with other males of the same species, as well as in attempts to ward off would-be predators.

This lurid, South African grasshopper is eating the shoots of euphorbia. It will acquire both food and toxins from the plant, the latter providing it with it a form of chemical defense. Its colors advertise its poisonous nature.

Following page: Viewed from this angle, the markings on the wings of this luna moth (Actias luna) resemble a comical, mustached face. Since the moth deliberately adopts this posture when threatened, it presumably confuses would-be attackers too!

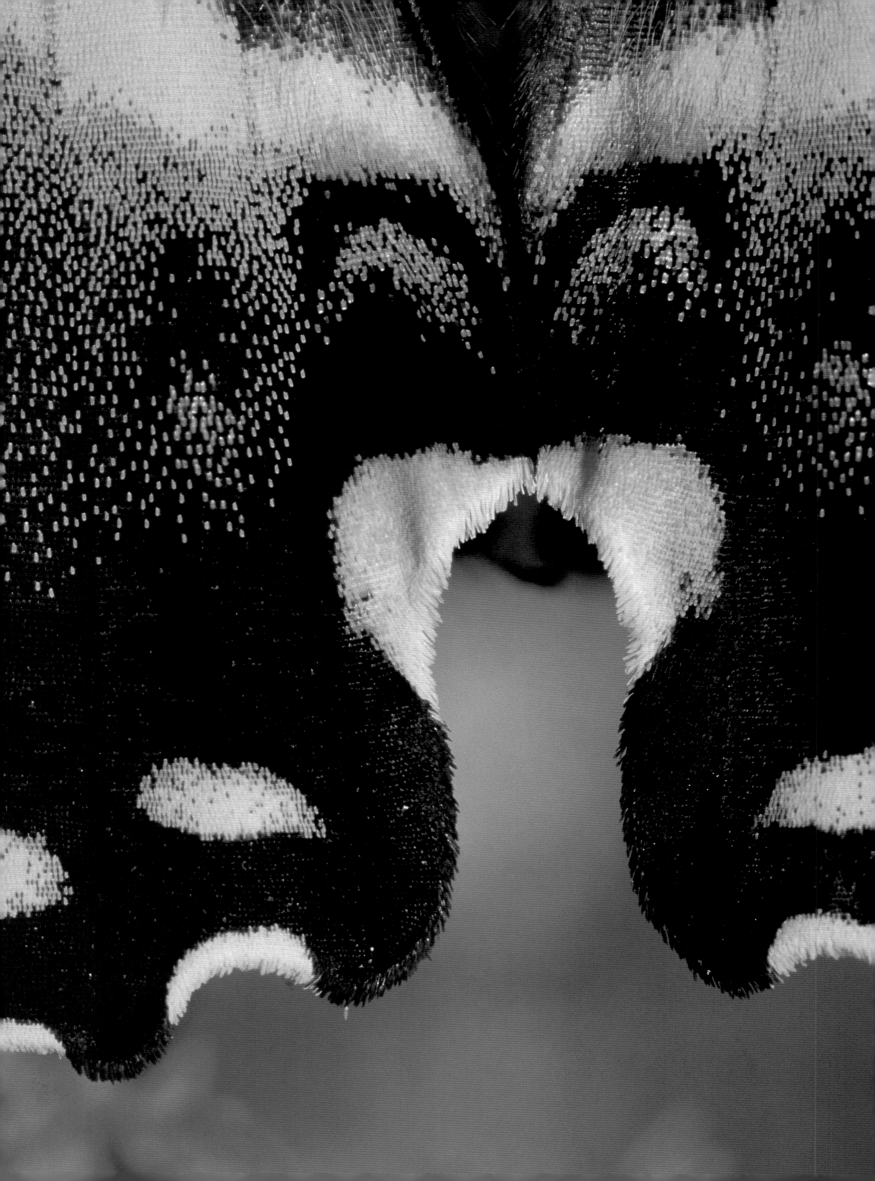

insect before discovering its toxicity. Most poisonous insects are brightly marked with orange or red to advertise the fact. Birds and mammals soon learn to associate these colors with distaste. Not surprisingly, insects with other means of defending themselves also employ warning colors. Wasps are a notable example of this. It should also come as no surprise that a number of harmless insects mimic the colors and markings of venomous and poisonous ones to escape the attention of predators.

Color, pattern and shape in defense

A few species use colors and patterns as bluff warnings or as distractions. Butterflies and moths are the best example of this. The eyed hawk moth (*Smerinthus ocellatus*) normally rests with its brown and gray fore wings covering its hind wings. If disturbed, however, it arches its abdomen and exposes large eye markings on the hind wings. These startle a would-be predator such as a bird, and discourage further attack.

Moths often use color and pattern on their wings as camouflage. Some species match the bark of a tree while others, such as the buff-tip (*Phalera bucephala*) look like broken twigs. In this case, the moth not only has the appropriate colors but also adopts a wing pose that enhances the deception. This mimicry of the natural world is at its extreme among the stick- and leaf-insects whose bodies resemble twigs and leaves. The leaf insects perfect this resemblance with their lifelike and seemingly random blemishes and holes (in fact, the wings and legs of the animal). Ironically, were these blemishes and holes in real leaves, the damage probably would have been caused insects.

To our eyes, the markings on the hind-wings of this palamedes swallowtail butterfly create a fanciful resemblance to a human face. Presumably this illusion is not wasted on the likes of potential predators.

Spot the insect! This superbly camouflaged katydid from Costa Rica not only mimics the colors of the mosses on which it lives, but has a texture to match as well. Movement is the only thing that would give its presence away.

Employing the services of others

Insects such as aphids are too small to defend themselves effectively from predators such as ladybirds. One survival technique is their vast numbers of offspring. Some more ingenious colonies of aphids employ the services of ants in their quest for survival. In return for protection, the aphids yield a sticky, sugary residue called honeydew which the ants find irresistible.

Homes

A few, select groups of insects protect themselves by building homes rather than by using stings, bites, or spines. This approach is largely the preserve of immature insect stages. The larvae of certain moths provide some good examples such as the oak leaf roller moth whose caterpillar, as its name implies, lives inside a rolled up leaf. The larvae of caddis flies have really turned this means of self defense into a way of life. Almost all of these home building insects are aquatic and the majority build cases in which they spend their entire larval lives. The building material used and the often unique construction methods employed depend on the species of insect. Grains of sand, twigs, plant leaves, or snail shells are all viable components.

As an insect group, moths display a wide range of camouflage patterns, often superb in their detail. This species from Ecuador has a striking resemblance to a dead leaf, shriveled along one of its margins.

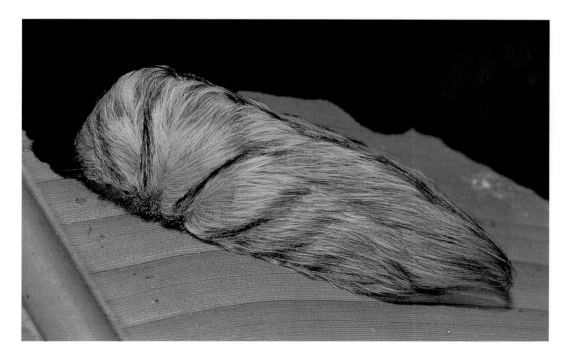

Tropical rainforest caterpillars often go to great lengths to deter the attentions of predators. Underneath the bizarre coating of fur-like hairs is a second line of defense in the form of poisonous spines.

Safety in numbers is a tactic employed by many insects, especially in their larval stages. These swallowtail butterfly caterpillars from the Amazon feed and rest together, producing unpleasant fluids if attacked.

The large, false eye markings on the thorax of this Ecuadorian click beetle serve to confuse potential predators by making the beetle look considerably more threatening than it really is.

STRANGE WAYS OF LIFE

Entomologists are usually attracted to their subject by the sheer variety and abundance of insects. From a purely aesthetic point of view, it is difficult to tire of a subject with seemingly endless shapes, colors, and appearances. Delve into the subject a little deeper, however, and an even more fascinating world exists in the behavior and life styles of insects. Although many life styles are rather conventional, some are nothing short of bizarre. The following is an account of some of the more intriguing of these.

Burying beetles

In a European woodland, within hours of a small mammal's death, its scent begins to waft on the breeze. Although extremely faint, burying beetles in the vicinity can detect the smell. When a male and female arrive on the scene, they immediately begin work digging beneath the corpse, gradually lowering it into a grave until it is buried several inches below the surface. Time is of the essence for the beetles because any delay may mean the arrival of a larger scavenger. Once the corpse is safely entombed in its subterranean chamber, the female beetle lays her eggs upon it. Both the adults and the subsequently hatched larvae then feed on the decomposing flesh.

Social insects

Although many insects lead rather solitary lives, some live in large and complex societies. Superficially, these are rather like idealized versions of our own society and comprise members with differing roles all working towards the good of the colony. Among the social insects, however, members of a colony are related. There is usually only one breeding female per colony and a limited number of fertile males. Most colony members are sterile and their roles confined to food collection and colony defense.

Bees and wasps are perhaps the most familiar social insects. They construct large nests with special chambers for the rearing of young and the storage of food. A typical honey bee (*Apis mellifera*) colony might

When a honeybee discovers a good supply of nectar and pollen, it informs other hive members upon its return to the colony. Details of distance and direction of the food source are relayed by means of a complex bee "dance."

Burying beetles are quick to capitalize on the death of a small mammal or bird. Attracted by the smell of decay, a pair meet up and quickly bury the corpse before laying their eggs alongside the entombed body.

Worker honeybees have special sacs attached to their hind legs. In these they are able to collect pollen from flowers and carry it back to the hive where it is used to feed developing larval bees.

As their name implies, these paper wasps are constructing their nest from chewed wood pulp, the end result closely resembling paper. Each cell in the nest will contain an egg, and subsequently a developing larval wasp.

Carpenter ants, like others of their kind, are extremely attentive to the colony's needs. Larvae are fed and tended and, together with the eggs and pupae, are defended to the death against attack.

Armed with an awesome set of jaws, this camponotus ant from Australia is not to be meddled with. Like many species of ants, when it bites an attacker it is extremely reluctant to let go.

comprise a single fertile queen who gives rise to around 50,000 sterile workers and a few sterile males, called drones. The queen mates once in her life and her sole function is to lay eggs over approximately five years. Construction and repair of the hive, care of the young, and the collection of food are the sole responsibilities of the worker bees. Each worker performs a different role at various times in its life. Intriguingly, a returning worker that has found a good source of nectar and pollen is able to communicate its distance and direction from the hive to other colony members through a strange dance.

Ants are among the most successful of all social insects and live in colonies like bees and wasps. Unlike their relatives, however, there are several different types of workers within a colony. Some workers collect food, others tend to the needs of the developing ant larvae, and the large-jawed ones act as soldiers and defend the colony.

Termites are common throughout the tropics and their imposing mounds, up to twenty feet high, are a testament to the enterprise of insect society. Within a termite colony, there are four types or 'castes': a queen, fertile males, and sterile workers and soldiers.

Gall wasps

Plants are an important source of food for all insects and, seemingly, all parts of a plant, from flower and leaf, to seed and root, are likely to be eaten by one insect or another. Not all relationships between plants and insects are straightforward, however, and no group better exemplifies this than the gall wasps. These tiny, superficially ant-like insects influence plants to produce abnormal growths called galls. Typically, the female gall wasp lays a single egg, or a collection depending on the species, inside plant tissue.

Upon hatching, the larvae induce swellings in the plant which eventually

become familiar galls. Galls serve both as food and protection for the wasp larvae which eventually pupate inside. Some species have life histories further complicated by the same alternating generations previously described in aphids: One generation requires the successful mating of separate males and females while the subsequent

The ways in which some insects exploit plant tissues are rather subtle. Certain wasps in particular are renowned for their ability to induce plant growths called galls in which their developing young feed and gain protection.

Leaf-cutter ants are abundant in tropical rainforests in Central and South America. Columns of ants progress across the forest floor and up trees, each returning to the colony bearing a neatly cut piece of leaf.

Ant colonies are ordered into distinct castes, each with different roles to play in the overall scheme of things. This winged queen is responsible for egg-laying while the smaller workers harvest food.

generation is parthenogenetic—females produce viable offspring without males.

Each species of gall wasp is usually restricted to a particular plant and produces a gall whose size, shape and color is also unique to that wasp. Species which alternate generations invariably produce different galls during the sexual and parthenogenetic stages in their lives.

Processionary moths

The caterpillars of certain moths sometimes walk along the ground in long lines, nose to tail. Species whose caterpillars engage in this behavior are generally referred to as processionary moths. One of the best known of these is the pine processionary moth of southern Europe. The caterpillars spend the daytime in large silken webs which they spin through the branches of trees. Irritating hairs from the caterpillars get caught in the web and combined with the silk, provide effective protection from predatory birds. At dusk, however, the caterpillars emerge on feeding forays. Following in a long line and retracing their silken path ensures that all the caterpillars can find their way back home.

Sloth moths

Three-toed sloths are strange, slow-moving creatures that live in the forests of Central and South America. Each animal has up to 100 sloth moths living in its coarse and matted fur. Each time the sloth climbs down a tree to visit its latrine on the ground, the moths lay their eggs in its dung. The caterpillars feed on the dung and pupate. The moths that subsequently emerge then fly off to find a new sloth.

AFTERWORD

INSECTS AND HUMAN BEINGS

Whether we like or not, insects of one sort or another affect our lives. They are with us in our homes and gardens, where we welcome some species more than others. In tropical countries, some are vectors for potentially fatal blood-borne diseases; while throughout the world, others are potentially serious pests of crops. Humans have found some positive ways to exploit a few species and are only now beginning to discover the beneficial effects of many others.

Whatever our feelings for insects, they touch our lives in countless ways. Entomologists find unlimited subjects for study in their vast numbers and seemingly endless shapes and forms. Even those who are indifferent to the functional elegance of insects would do well to remember their overall environmental importance. Specifically, insects play a pivotal role in the food webs and ecology of almost all terrestrial and freshwater ecosystems. Stated simply, we need a healthy environment for our own survival and the abundance and diversity of insect life on the planet not only reflect that state of the environment, but are integral to its continued well-being.

Termites are famous for the huge colonial mounds that they create, some of which are far taller than a man. Each termite species produces mounds of unique proportions. This mound was photographed in Namibia.

INDEX

*Page numbers in **bold-face** type indicate photo captions.*

abdomens, 7–10, 20
anatomy of insects, 7–10
  body structure, 20
  exoskeletons, 22
  of internal organs, 22
  legs, 46
  mouthparts, 37–38
  for movement, 45
  of promethia moths, **7**
  for self-defense, 53
  wings, 49
Anoplura, 14
antennae, 20
anthropods, 7
aphids, 34, 60, 69–70
aquatic insects, 46, 60,
assassin bugs, 37

bean beetles, **29**
bees
  as social insects, 65–69
  stings by, 54
  see also honey bees
behavior
  of processionary moths, 70
  reproductive, 33–34
  of social insects, 65–69
  swarming, 26
bioluminescent insects, 33, 34
birds, insects as food for, 53
bombardier beetles (*Brachinus*), 54
book lice, 14
brains of insects, 22
buff-tip moths (*Phalera bucephala*), 59
burying beetles, 65, **65**
bush-crickets, 14, 26
butterflies, 17
  as caterpillars, 38, 53
  coloration of, 59
  heliconius butterflies, **42**
  lacewing butterflies, **49**
  larval stages of, 30
  monarch butterflies, **30**
  mouthparts of, **37**
  owl butterflies, **13**
  palamedes swallowtail butterflies, 59
  peacock butterflies, **18**
  pupal stage of, 30
  swallowtail butterflies, **62**
  wings of, 49

caddis flies, 17
camouflage
  of caterpillars, 30
  of ghost walker beetles, **17**
  of giant stick insects, **13**
  of jagged ambush bugs, **20**
  of katydids, 53, **59**
  of leaf insects, **22**
  of moths, 59, **61**
  of thornbugs, **4**
  of tortoise beetles, **11**
camponotus ants, **67**
carnivorous insects, 37–39
carpenter ants, **67**
caterpillars, 30, 53
  camouflage by, **61**
  of death's-head sphinx moths, **33**
  feeding by, 38
  of io moths, **54**
  of oak leaf roller moths, 60
  of processionary moths, 70
  self-defense by, **60**
  of sloth moths, 70
  of swallowtail butterflies, **62**
  chemical defenses, 54
Chordates, 7
cicadas, seventeen-year, **14**
citrus root weevils, **25**
classification of insects, 7–10
  with complete metamorphosis, 17
  with partial metamorphosis, 14
  of primitive wingless insects, 10
click beetles, **62**
cockroaches, 14
Coleoptera, 17
Collembola, 10
colonies of social insects, 65–69
coloration, 59
  of poisonous insects, 38, 55, 59
  of wings, 49
  see also camouflage
crickets, 14, **17**
cynthia moths, 50, 70

damselflies, 7, 14, 26
death's-head sphinx moths (*Acherontia atropos*), **33**
Dermaptera, 14
Dictyoptera, 14
diet, 38–39
  see also feeding
digestive systems of insects, 22
Diplura, 10
Diptera, 17
diving beetles (*Dyticus*), 37, 46, **46**
dragonflies, 7, 14, **49**
  fossils of, 4
  halloween pennant dragonflies, 50
  nymph stages of, 26, 46
  Odonata, **33**

earwigs, 14
eggs, 26, 30
  of bean beetles, **29**
  laid in mammal corpses, 65, **65**
  of praying mantids, **29**
  of queen bees, 69
  of sloth moths, 70
  of tiger swallowtails, **26**
Embioptera, 14
entomologists, 10

Ephemeropter, 14
exoskeletons, 7, **17**, 22, 53
eyed hawk moths (*Smerinthus ocellatus*), 59
eye markings, 59, **62**
eyes of insects, 20, **21**

feeding, 37
  diets, 38–39
  by honey bees, dance for, **65**
  mouthpart adaptations for, 37–38
female insects, 33
field crickets, **17**
fireflies (*Lampyridae*), 33
fleas, 17
flies, 17
  feeding by, 39
  wings of, 49
flowers
  nectar produced by, 39
  pollinated by insects, **4**, **42**
flying, 49, 45
fossils of insects, 4
funny face katydids, **42**

gall wasps, 69, 69–70
ghost walker beetles, **17**
giant robber flies, **39**
giant stick insects, **13**
giant water bugs, **29**
glow-worms, 34
grasshoppers, 14
  chemical defenses by, **55**
  eggs of, 26
  leaping by, **46**
  legs of, 46
  lubber grasshoppers, **39**
  lumber grasshoppers, **14**
  nymph stages of, **4**
great diving beetles, 37

habitats, 4
halloween pennant dragonflies, 50
harlequin beetles, **13**
hawkmoths, 50
  eyed hawk moths, 59
  larval stages of, 34
heads, 7, 20
  of lumber grasshoppers, **14**
heliconius butterflies (*Heliconiidae*), **42**
Hemiptera, 14
honey bees (*Apis mellifera*)
  colonies of, 65–69
  dance of, **65**
  flying by, 45
  legs of, 46
  pollen collected by, 66
horseflies, **21**, 39
humans, insects and, 71
Hymenoptera, 17

instars, 30
internal organs of insects, 22
io moths, **54**
Isoptera, 14

jagged ambush bugs, **20**

katydids, **53**
  camouflage by, **59**
  feeding by, **42**
  funny face katydids, **42**

lacewing butterflies, **49**
ladybugs (*Coccinella*), **26**, 53
larval stages, 30
  caterpillars as, 38
  of death's-head sphinx moths, *33*
  of gall wasps, 69
  of hawkmoths, 34
  homes of insects in, 60
  see also caterpillars
leaf-cutter ants, 69
leaf insects, 14, **22**, 59
leaf-miners, 38
leaping, 46, **46**
leaves, as food, 38
legs of insects, 45, 46
Lepidoptera, 17
lice, 14
life cycles, 25
  of aphids, 34, 69–70
  complete metamorphosis in, 26–30
  partial metamorphosis in, 25–26
  of seventeen-year cicadas, 14
lubber grasshoppers, **39**
lumber grasshoppers (*Brachystola magna*), **14**
luna moths (*Actias luna*), **55**

male insects, 33
Mallophaga, 14
mantidfly (*Mantispidae*), **22**
mating, *see reproduction*
mayflies, 14
Mecoptera, 17
metamorphosis, 25
  complete, 17, 26–30
  partial, 14, 25–26
migrations, flying for, 49
mole-crickets (*Gryllotalpa*), 46
molting, 22, 30
monarch butterflies (*Danaus plexipus*), **30**
  caterpillar stage of, **34**
  migrations of, 49
mosquitoes, 39
mouths
  adaptations of, for feeding, 37–38
  of camponotus ants, **67**
  of moths and butterflies, **37**
  of praying mantids, 38
  used in self-defense, 54
movement, 45–49

mud-dauber wasps, **11**

nectar, as food, 39, 42
nests of insects, 60
  of paper wasps, 66
  termite mounds, 69, 71
Neuroptera, 17
nymph stages, 25, 26
  of assassin bugs, 37
  of dragonflies, 46
  of grasshoppers, 4

oak leaf roller moths, 60
Odonata, 14, **33**
Orthoptera, 14
owl butterflies, **13**

painted lady butterflies (*Vanessa cardui*), 49
palamedes swallowtail butterflies, 59
paper wasps, 66
parthenogenesis, 34
peacock butterflies, **18**
Phasmida, 14
pheromones, 33
Phyla, 7
pine processionary moths, 70
plants
  as food, 38–39
  gall wasps and, 69–70, **69**
  pollinated by insects, 42
Plecoptera, 14
poisonous insects, 38, 54–59, 55
praying mantids (*Mantis*)
  anatomy of, **22**
  egg cases of, 26, **29**
  feeding by, **38**
  hunting and feeding by, 45
  legs of, 46
  mating behavior of, **30**
  threat display of, 53
predators
  of insects, 53, 60
  insects as, **45**
primitive wingless insects, 10, 25, 33–34
proboscis, **37**
processionary moths, 70
promethia moths (*Callosamia promethia*), **7**
Protura, 10
Psocoptera, 14
pupal stage, 30, **30**

queen bees, 69

reproduction, 33–34
  by citrus root weevils, **25**
  of gall wasps, 69–70
  by parthenogenesis, 34
  by social insects, 69
respiration in insects, 22
rhinoceros beetles (*Dynastes*), **55**
robber flies, **18**

scorpion flies, 17
self-defense, 53
  alliances for, 60
  chemical defenses, 54
  coloring, patterns and shapes for, 59
  hard bodies for, 53
  insect architecture for, 60
  physical defenses, 54
  poisons for, 54–59
seventeen-year cicadas (*Magicicada septendecim*), **14**
sexes, 33–34
sexual dimorphism, 33
Siphonaptera, 17
sloth moths, 70
sloths, 70
social insects, 65–69
species of insects, 3
spermatophores, 33
spiderflies, **42**
springtails, 10
stick insects, 14, 59
stings, 54
stoneflies, 14
swallowtail butterflies, **62**
swarming, **26**
swimming, 46, **46**

taxony, 7
termites, 14
  mounds of, **71**
  as social insects, 69
thoraxes, 7, 20
thornbugs, **4**
thrips, 14
Thysanoptera, 14
Thysanura, 10
tiger swallowtails (*Papilio glaucus*), **26**
tortoise beetles, **11**
toxic poisons, 54–59
Trichoptera, 17
true bugs, 14, 39
true flies, 49

warblers (*Sylviidae* and *Parulidae*), 53
water beetles, 46
water boatman (*Notonecta*), **17**, 46
water bugs, **29**
water stick-insects (*Ranatra*), 46
web-spinners, 14
weevils (*Curcullionidae*), 10
  citrus root weevils, **25**
wingless insects, 10
wings, 7, 49
  of beetles, **3**
  eye markings on, 59
wood
  as food, 38–39
  nests built of, 66